Little Pebble™

Colorful Foods

Orange Foods

by Martha E. H. Rustad

CAPSTONE PRESS
a capstone imprint

Little Pebble is published by Capstone Press,
1710 Roe Crest Drive, North Mankato, Minnesota 56003
www.mycapstone.com

Library of Congress Cataloging-in-Publication Data
Names: Rustad, Martha E. H. (Martha Elizabeth Hillman), 1975– author.
Title: Orange foods / by Martha E. H. Rustad.
Description: North Mankato, Minnesota : Capstone Press, [2017] | Series:
Little pebble. Colorful foods | Audience: Ages 4–7. | Audience: K to grade 3. | Includes bibliographical references and index.
Identifiers: LCCN 2016009744| ISBN 9781515723707 (library binding) | ISBN 9781515723745 (pbk.) | ISBN 9781515723783 (ebook (pdf))
Subjects: LCSH: Food—Juvenile literature. | Orange (Color)—Juvenile literature. | Color of food—Juvenile literature.
Classification: LCC TX355 .R855 2017 | DDC 641.3—dc23
LC record available at http://lccn.loc.gov/2016009744

Editorial Credits
Megan Atwood, editor; Juliette Peters, designer;
Jo Miller, media researcher; Steve Walker, production specialist

Photo Credits
Images by Capstone Studio: Karon Dubke
Photo styling: Sarah Schuette and Marcy Morin

Printed and bound in China

PO007712LEOF16

Table of Contents

Orange Foods. 4

Orange Fruits 6

Orange Vegetables 12

Orange Meals. 18

Glossary 22
Read More 23
Internet Sites 23
Index. 24

Orange Foods

How does orange taste?

Let's find out.

Orange Fruits

Eat a peach.

It is shiny inside.

Peel an orange.

It is sweet.

Apricots are small.

They make good snacks.

Yum!

Orange Vegetables

Carrots grow in rows.

Crunch!

I bite hard.

A pumpkin gets big.

Put it in soup.

Yams have skin.

We bake them.

Hot!

Orange Meals

We eat grilled cheese.

The cheese drips.

Dad grills salmon.
I help him.

What other foods
are orange?

Glossary

salmon—a fish that lives part of its life in the ocean and part of its life in streams

shiny—giving off light

vine—a long stem

yam—a vegetable that grows underground

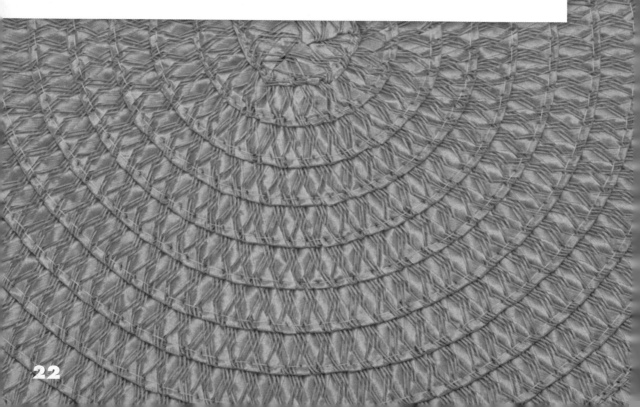

Read More

O'Connell, Emma. *We Love Orange!* Our Favorite Colors. New York: Gareth Stevens Publishing, 2016.

Rustad, Martha E. H. *Orange.* Colors in Nature. Minneapolis: Bullfrog Books, 2014.

Stevens, Madeline. *Orange Around Me.* Color in My World. New York: Cavendish Square, 2015.

Internet Sites

FactHound offers a safe, fun way to find Internet sites related to this book. All of the sites on FactHound have been researched by our staff.

Here's all you do:
Visit *www.facthound.com*
Type in this code: 9781515723707

Index

apricots, 10
carrots, 12
cheese, 18
grilled cheese, 18
peach, 6
pumpkin, 14
salmon, 20
skin, 16
snacks, 10
soup, 14
yams, 16